BIRDS OF WEST AFRICA

A CHILD'S GUIDE

Virginia W Dike

Illustrated by Robin Gowen

CASSAVA REPUBLIC

New edition published by Cassava Republic Press 2023
Revised edition published by Cassava Republic Press 2011
First published by Fourth Dimension Publishing Co Ltd 1986

Text © Virginia W Dike
Illustration © Robin M Gowen

Cover design by John Hawkins

A CIP catalogue record for this book is available from the
National Library of Nigeria and the British Library.

Nigerian ISBN: 978-1-913175-43-6
British ISBN: 978-1-913175-43-6

Printed in Czech Republic by Akcent Media Limited

Visit us at www.cassavarepublic.biz

CONTENTS

INTRODUCING BIRDS

Birds are animals with feathers. They have two wings, and most birds can fly. They flap their wings to rise in the air. Their feathers, strong chest muscles and light bones help them to fly. Scientists believe that birds evolved long ago from small flying dinosaurs. Like human beings and other mammals, birds are warm-blooded vertebrates (animals with backbones).

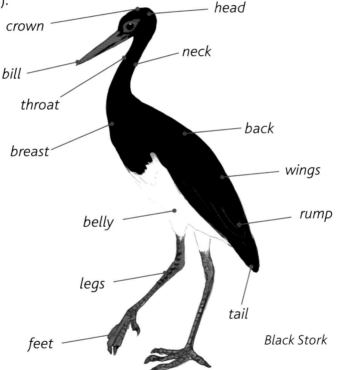

crown
head
bill
neck
throat
breast
back
wings
belly
rump
legs
tail
feet
Black Stork

Birds hatch from eggs. They build nests to hold the eggs until they hatch. A nest can be made of woven grass, a pile of sticks, or feathers stuck to a wall. It can even be a hole in the ground. When the eggs hatch, the parents feed and care for the baby birds.

HOW TO LOOK AT BIRDS

People find that they can get more enjoyment out of seeing birds when they can identify the species they are looking at. At first it can be confusing, but don't worry. All you need to get started are these basic guidelines on how to look at birds. Birds are different from each other in the way they look, the way they act, and the places they stay. These things will help you tell one bird from another.

Birds differ in appearance.
They are different sizes – from very large, to very small.

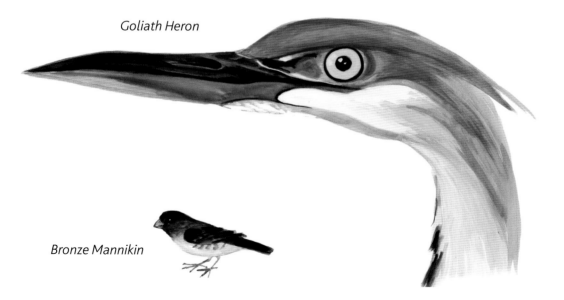

Goliath Heron

Bronze Mannikin

Birds differ in colour. They may be one colour or many, bright or dull.

Senegal Coucal   *Barn Owl*

Birds differ in shape. They can be plump like a quail or slender like a Jacana. They can have a long or short neck, long or short tail, long or short legs.

Their bills have different shapes, depending on the food they eat.

Crimson Seed-cracker
Seeds

Sunbird
Nectar

Tit
Insects

Senegal Parrot
Nuts

Saddlebill Stork
Fish

Great Blue Plantain-eater
Fruit

Birds' feet are different in sizes and are shaped for different purposes.

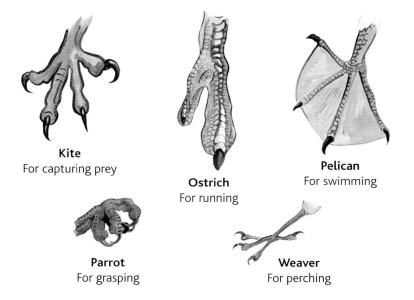

Kite
For capturing prey

Ostrich
For running

Pelican
For swimming

Parrot
For grasping

Weaver
For perching

Birds are different in behaviour. They may be active or quiet, graceful or awkward, noisy or still. Some birds are always singing and chattering, while others are not heard. One bird may sit in plain view, while another hides in the grass.

Some birds stay alone, while others move about together. Some birds stay in pairs, especially when they are building a nest and raising their young.

Birds live in different places.
They may live near water,
in the forest,
in the savanna,
and in town.

Birds perch in trees,
hide in the grass,
run on the ground,
fly from tree to tree,
soar high in the sky.

The following pages describe some of the birds of West Africa, with Hausa (H), Igbo (I) and Yoruba (Y) names. Find out what they look like, how they behave, and where they can be found. Then look carefully. Through these pages you will begin to discover the many wonderful birds of West Africa.

PLANTAIN-EATER
Violet Plantain-eater

Okpoko (I)   Kolekole (Y)   Kulkulu (H)

Bright birds fill the forest — violet, green, red, blue, yellow. They are Plantain-eaters or Turacos, a family of large, colourful birds found only in Africa. While the Grey Plantain-eater is seen everywhere, its colourful cousins live deep in the forest. The Violet Plantain-eater has a purple body, with red under the wings. And what an amazing face — like a clown! The face is a patchwork of red, orange and white. The bill is a big yellow triangle with a red tip.

The Plantain-eaters hop, leap, spring, and bound along the branches, eating fruit. They fly to the next tree with a few flaps and a glide. One cries out a loud *Courou, courou, courou!* Another takes up the call and others join the chorus, echoing through the forest loud and clear.

PARROT
Grey Parrot

Icheoku (I)   Ayekooto, Ode (Y)   Aku (H)

Parrots live in the forest, high up in the trees. Grey Parrots have a grey body and red tail. They have big heads and strong curved bills. Their bills are useful for climbing trees and cracking nuts. Parrots eat nuts, fruits, and seeds – but they like oil palm kernels best of all.

Parrots are noisy birds. How they squawk as they fly! Some people keep Parrots as pets. They can learn to say many words. Have you ever heard a pet Parrot talk?

WOODPECKER
Fire-bellied Woodpecker

Otulukpokpo (I)   Akoko (Y)   Makokofa (H)

High in a forest tree a Fire-bellied Woodpecker is tapping. It has a bright red belly and black and white on its sides.

Have you ever heard a Woodpecker tapping? They tap the tree trunk looking for food. They cut holes in the wood with their sharp straight bills. They bring out insects with their long sticky tongues. Their special feet, claws and tail help them climb straight up and down. Up and down they go, tapping for food.

SUNBIRD
Collared Sunbird

Nza (I)   Aroni (Y)   Sha-kauci (H)

Look in the garden! See the tiny bird darting from flower to flower. Its green head and back shine in the sunlight. It is a Collared Sunbird.

Some sunbirds have long curved bills and hollow tongues for eating nectar from flowers. The Collared Sunbird has a shorter bill and especially likes to eat small insects.

Sunbirds are very active, even in the hot sun. They fly about the garden. They cling to a flower or hover in the air to feed. All day long they dart about – always active, never still.

BULBUL
Garden Bulbul

Ochiri, Okiri (I)   Opera (Y)   Koji, Jan Gaba (H)

Some birds attract notice with their beautiful colours – but not the Garden Bulbul. It is dark grey, dull brown and dirty white.

The Garden Bulbul attracts attention by its noise. Early in the morning the Bulbuls start to sing. They sing all day. Hear the Bulbuls chatter as they chase birds from a perch – or scold hawks and snakes. Singing, chattering, scolding – the Bulbul is never quiet.

Why is the Bulbul in the garden? Their favourite foods are bright peppers, sweet berries, ripe cashews, and grasshoppers for their young.

KINGFISHER
Pigmy Kingfisher

Nkene (I)   Yojayoja (Y)   Cinawuya (H)

The Pigmy Kingfisher is a tiny beautiful bird – bright blue above and orange below. Its bill and feet are red. Like other Kingfishers, the Pigmy has a straight bill, thick body, and short legs and tail. Also like many Kingfishers, it does not eat fish or live near water.

You may see the Pigmy Kingfisher perched on a wire or branch. It raises its head up and down, up and down. It is looking for food. Suddenly it dives into the grass. It flies up with a grasshopper, beetle, or frog. It dives into puddles too, but only to enjoy a bath.

THRUSH
Kurrikane Thrush

Pakoko (Y)   Cizar, Alafa, Wani irin tsuntsu (H)

Early in the morning the Thrush begins to sing: "Pretty one, pretty one, pretty one! Wake up! Wake up!" Over and over they sing, never stopping to rest.

Thrushes have a bright yellow bill and plain brown body. They are light grey below with orange under the wings.

Thrushes hunt on the ground. Cocking the head, they look for juicy worms and crunchy insects. Quickly they run to make a catch. In the dry season, thrushes feast on ripe cashew and mangoes that fall to the ground.

ROLLER
Broad-billed Roller

Oroghoro (I)   Polongo (Y)   Ladan (H)

The Broad-billed Roller squawks, squawks from its high perch. It swoops down to chase off crows and kites. It makes such a racket!

High up the Broad-billed Roller looks purple-brown, a stocky bird with a big head and bright yellow bill. But as it flies, bright blue wings and tail appear. It flies fast like a falcon. At evening Rollers wheel about overhead, catching insects in the air.

As the dry season ends, male and female sit side by side. He flies off and returns with a juicy insect treat. When she accepts, he brings another gift. Soon there will be a nest and eggs and young ones to feed.

SWALLOW
European Swallow

Ayoro (I)   Alapandede (Y)   Alallaka, Kabdodo (H)

Some birds live in West Africa year round; others migrate here for part of the year. European Swallows migrate to Africa for the dry season, when the weather is cold in Europe. They fly to Africa where they will find warm weather and plenty of insects to eat. In April they migrate back to Europe.

Swallows can be seen lined up on a wire – or darting over a field catching insects. They swoop down to drink from puddles. They fly with long curved wings and a forked tail.

WEAVER
Village Weaver

Ahia (I)   Ega (Y)   Marai (H)

What a racket in the big tall tree! Hundreds of weaver birds have made their colony. The noisy yellow birds cluster round the nests. They hang from nests, which hang from branches, all over the tree.

Chitter-chatter! Chitter-chatter! fills the village square. Nests must be built; nests must be repaired. So to and fro, to and fro they go. Flashes of yellow and black fly from nest to palm tree. Back they go from palm tree to nest, carrying bits of palm in their bills.

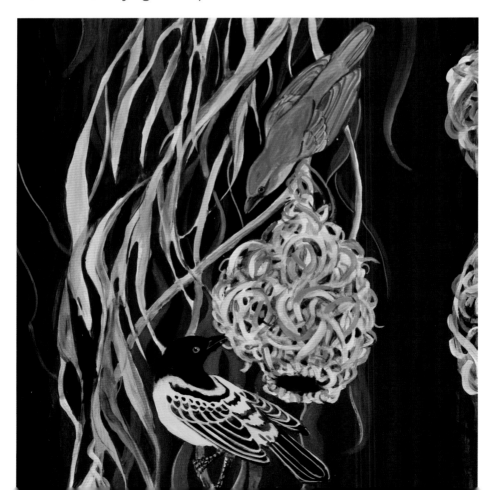

CUCKOO
Didric Cuckoo

Kpalakuku (I)   Ajemayo (Y)   Tsuntsu (H)

A haunting call comes from high in the tree – *Di- di- di- deea- deea! Di- di- di- deea- deea!* Over and over the Didric Cuckoo cries, as if calling us away to a far off land.

Now the Didric Cuckoo comes down to the garden. See a bright green and white bird with a red eye – shiny green and bronze above, spotted with white.

Cuckoos do not raise their young. Didric Cuckoos lay their eggs in a Weaver bird's nest –and leave the Weavers to raise their young.

HORNBILL
Allied Hornbill

Opiopio (I)   Atiala (Y)   Hankaka-Mogoli (H)

The Allied Hornbill looks a bit odd. It is a large black and white bird with a long tail and an ENORMOUS bill. Hornbills are often seen feeding in tall trees or flying high overhead.

The Hornbill is not a graceful bird. It bobs up and down eating fruit in the treetops. It flaps from tree to tree trying to catch insects as it flies. It makes loud, laughing noises, rocking its whole body when it calls. A funny awkward bird is the Hornbill!

COUCAL
Senegal Coucal

Ovu (I)   Elulu (Y)   Dan-Ragowa (H)

The Senegal Coucal is a handsome bird. It has a black head and tail, chestnut brown wings, and a white belly. It is medium large with a broad tail.

Where does one look for the Senegal Coucal? Not in the air, for this bird does not fly very well. It flaps over the road and falls into a bush. It walks through the tall grass hunting grasshoppers and lizards. But even though Coucals look weak, they are known for killing snakes.

Have you heard the Coucal call? It sounds like water bubbling out of a bottle — *Hu-Hu-Hu-Hu-Hu-Hu-Hu-Hu*.

EGRET
Cattle Egret

Ubala (I)   Lekeleke (Y)   Balbela (H)

Everyone knows the Cattle Egret. It is a large white bird with long legs, a long neck and a long bill. When you see a herd of cattle, you will often see Cattle Egrets nearby. They eat the insects that fly up as the cattle walk.

Most Egrets are found near water, but the Cattle Egret is found everywhere. In the dry season they spread over the land. During the rains, they fly to northern Nigeria to breed. Some have even flown across the Atlantic Ocean and now live in far away America. They fly in a V-pattern with their heads pulled back and feet dangling behind.

CROW
Pied Crow

Ugolo-oma (I)   Kanakana (Y)   Hankaka (H)

The Pied Crow is a large black bird with a white collar. They are usually seen in pairs or in groups with Vultures and Kites. Crows chase each other in the air or go after small hawks. *Kaa, kaa*, the crow cries as it flies overhead. *Croak*, it calls in a low voice.

Most birds eat one special kind of food—seeds or insects or fruit. The Pied Crow eats almost everything! Dead animals, young birds, eggs, palm fruits, insects, lizards, termites, garbage – the Pied Crow eats them all!

GUINEA-FOWL
Helmeted Guinea-fowl

Ogaze (I)   Awo (Y)   Zabo (H)

Guinea-fowl cover the hillside in the early morning light. They are large birds with round bodies and small heads. They have grey-black feathers speckled with white. But their heads have no feathers at all – only rough patches of red and blue skin.

These birds rarely fly but are great runners and walkers. They eat many foods – seeds, fruits, leaves, worms, insects, snails, lizards and snakes.

Guinea-fowl live in the wild, but they are also domestic animals. They are valued for their eggs and tasty meat. They also eat ticks that carry disease and their cries warn farmers of danger at night.

VULTURE
Hooded Vulture

Udele (I)   Igun (Y)   Angulu (H)

The Vulture is an ugly bird. It has no feathers on its head and neck. It walks with an awkward limp.

Vultures are ugly but useful. They have strong bills and sharp claws, which help them eat dead animals. In this way scavengers like the Vulture keep the land clean.

Look around next time a fowl or goat is killed. See the Vultures gather. They circle in the air. They sit on the rooftops. They wait. They will eat whatever is left behind.

25

KITE
Black Kite

Egbe (I)   Asa, Awodi (Y)   Shirwa (H)

This is the world's most common bird of prey. It is found on four continents—Africa, Asia, Europe and Australia. Black Kites are actually plain brown. They have wide-spread wings and a forked tail, strong claws and a hooked bill. The Kite swoops down to catch small animals—chicks and mice, lizards and frogs.

See the Kite in the air. How gracefully it flies! It dives to the ground and climbs up high. It spreads its wings and glides. It flies, its wingtips spread like fingers. It tilts its tail to change direction. How gracefully it flies!

OWL
White-faced Owl

Okwukwuu (I) Owiwi (Y) Mujiya (H)

Kuk-kuuu, kuk-kuuu calls an Owl in the darkness. Quietly it perches on a tree or roof. Silently it flies out to hunt. Most birds are active during the day, but Owls come out at night.

The White-faced Owl has a grey and brown body. It has a big head and large yellow eyes. Its eyes, like those of people, are set looking forward.

Owls have strong claws and a hooked bill. They hunt mice and insects. During a bush fire, owls rush to catch small animals as they run out.

SWIFT
Little African Swift

Elo, Eneke (I)   Olofere (Y)   Tsattwewa (H)

The Little African Swift is always in the air. Over the housetops they circle and squeal, *Creee, creee*. High in the church ceiling they fly round and round, never stopping to rest.

The Little African Swift is black with a white throat and rump. It has long curved wings. The Swift flies most of the day. Its wings are strong but its feet are weak. The Swift clings to trees or buildings, but it never comes to the ground.

Swifts even eat in the air. They open their mouths wide and catch insects as they fly.

PIGEON
Green Fruit Pigeon

Ndoh (I)   Ako, Orofo (Y)   Kurchiyar-Gamji (H)

Green birds with red and blue bills fill the tall fruit tree. These are Green Fruit Pigeons. They are green and they love to eat fruit! Wild figs are their favourite.

Pigeons, like their relatives the doves, are heavy birds with small heads. They fly very fast. High in the tree the birds sit eating fruit. Their colour matches the leaves so they cannot easily be seen.

Then comes a loud *whirrr*. Off they zoom together, like a squadron of jet planes in flight, leaving behind an empty tree.

PIPIT
Yellow-throated Long-claw

Barawe (Y)

Two streaked brown birds are hidden in the grass. They run, stop – run, stop. But look! The same bird has a bright yellow breast with a broad black U. Always in pairs, the Yellow-throated Long-claws fly up to a tree. They perch on the very top, calling out a loud *Twee-oo! Twee-oo!*

Then the two fly off, gently rising and falling – flutter-flutter-glide, flutter-flutter-glide. Hear their sweet song as they fly – *Hee-ro-weet! Hee-ro-weet*! Rising and gliding, rising and gliding. Then gently down. They land, displaying white as they spread their tails.

MANNIKIN
Bronze Mannikin

Oori (Y)

Chrreep, chrreep, chrreep, the tiny birds call as they swing on the grass. *Chrreep, chrreep,* they sing as they fly from bush to bush. Busy, busy, they pick seeds from the ground. Flick, flick go wings and tails as they splash in puddles.

Bronze Mannikins are tiny birds, dark above and white below. They like to travel in groups, twittering as they go. In puddles, on the ground, in the air, on bushes and grass – together they go. *Chrreep, chrreep, chrreep.*

WHYDAH
Pin-tailed Whydah

Ibarra, Nnundo Chukwu (I) Ologose (Y) Zalaidu (H)

The male Pin-tailed Whydah easily attracts notice. He is the small black and white bird with a red bill and very long tail! His tail is even longer than his body. When he flies it bobs up and down behind him.

But what of the female Whydah? She is the small brown bird nearby. The male hovers over her, bobbing his tail and flicking his wings. He sings. He displays. He is trying to attract a mate. His dance in the air is for her, but she seems not to notice he is there.

FINCH
Senegal Fire Finch

Chiri-Igeri (I)   Ologiri (Y)   Bawan-Allah (H)

The male Fire Finch is bright red; the female is mostly brown. Finches are small birds with short wide bills. They use their bills to crack open the seeds they eat. They hop about, picking seeds from the ground.

The Senegal Fire Finch does not fear people. They come into the compound and garden to look for food. They may even enter houses or come into a shop to take rice. They often build their nests in a thatched roof or grass wall. So look for a Fire Finch – one might be very close by!

Many other birds live in West Africa and around the world. The following activities will help you see and enjoy more birds wherever you may be.

Attract birds to your garden

Birds need places to live and food to eat. You can help create a more bird-friendly environment with the following activities:

- Help plant trees and shrubs in your garden. These give birds places to perch and shelter, find food, and build their nests.

- Attract birds to your compound with fruit trees like cashew and mango.

- Plant flowers; birds like to sip the sweet nectar. They also eat the insects that feed on flowers.

- Create places for birds to bathe and drink water. You can build a simple bird bath with a shallow basin on a stand. Be careful to put it out of reach of cats and other animals who like to feed on birds.

- Make a bird feeder when food is scarce. Use a coconut shell or gourd hung from a branch or a tray outside the window. Fill these with seeds, grains like rice and corn, or suet (the heavy white fat from animals). Beware of cats when placing the feeder!

- Help birds build nests. You can do this by putting nesting materials in a shrub or basket hung from a tree. Birds use materials like twigs, string and yarn, small bits of cloth, hair, wood shavings, paper, and cotton in building their nests.

It's mating season for birds

- Many birds mate and nest in the rainy season.

- Have you seen any birds mating?

- Have you seen them building nests?

- Have you seen any baby birds?

- Watch for male birds that change to bright colours in the mating season (Whydahs, Bishops, Finches).

- Watch for courtship displays (like that of the Pin-tailed Whydah).

- Listen for courtship songs (like that of the Thrush).

- Watch for a male bird giving food gifts to the female (Rollers and Kingfishers do this).

- Watch for birds carrying materials for building their nests (Weavers, Crows).

- Watch for nests hidden in the shrubs (Sunbirds) or high in a tree (Kites).

- Watch for birds guarding their nest.

- Watch for birds bringing food to their young.

- In watching nests, be careful not to come so close as to frighten the mother and father birds away.

- Watch for parents teaching their young ones to fly.

- Keep a nature journal

Make a record of birds and other animals you see, writing about them and drawing their pictures in a nature journal. The following checklist will help you.

BIRD OBSERVATION CHECKLIST

- Bird's name

- Where did you see the bird?

- What did the bird look like?

- What was its size? Was the bird:

Tiny	like a Sunbird, Finch, Pigmy Kingfisher	(10 cm./4 in.)
Small	like a Swallow, Bulbul, Weaver	(13-20 cm./5-8 in.)
Medium	like a Thrush, Dove, Roller	(23-30 cm. / 9-12 in.)
Large	like a Coucal, Hornbill, Crow	(36-50 cm./14-20 in.)
Very large	like a Vulture, Guinea-fowl, Stork	(60+ cm. /23+ in.)

- What was the shape of the body? Was it slender or plump?

- Was the neck long or short? What of the legs? The bill? The tail?

- Was the bill straight or curved, narrow or broad?

- Was the tail broad like a fan? Shaped like a fork?

- Were the wings straight or curved?

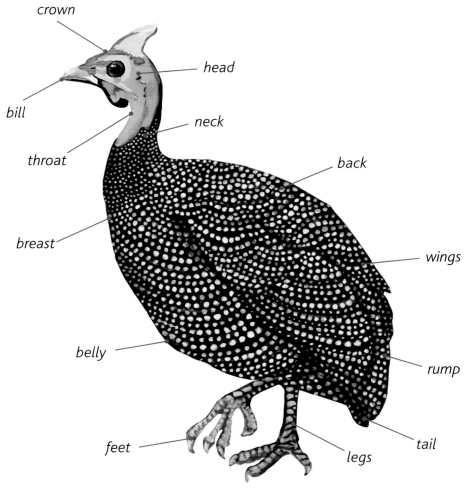

crown

head

bill

neck

throat

back

breast

wings

belly

rump

feet

legs

tail

Guinea Fowl

• What were the bird's colours? Birds come in all colours. The shade can be light or dark, shiny or dull. Two colours can also be combined, as in blue-green, orange-brown.

white   black   grey   brown   orange   red   yellow   green   blue   purple

• Describe the colour of the head, breast, belly, back, wings, tail, bill, eye, feet, etc.

• Did male and female birds look the same or different?

• What was the bird doing? Did it hop on the ground, fly from tree to tree, walk in the grass, fly high in the sky, sit on a perch? Was it easy to see or hidden?

• Did the bird flap its wings, turn its tail, move its neck, ruffle its feathers?

• Was it noisy or quiet? What kind of noise did it make? Was it singing?

• Was the bird alone? Was it moving, feeding, playing, chasing or fighting with another bird?

• Was the bird eating? Was it trying to get food? What kind of food?

• Add any other questions you can think of.

• **And keep looking for birds around you!**

GUIDE FOR PARENTS AND EDUCATORS

Birds offer children a gateway to the natural world because they are everywhere. Bird watching fosters appreciation of the beauty of nature and interdependence of all forms of life, while also enabling children to develop vital learning skills. It furthers a spirit of inquiry and creativity, encourages self-directed learning, and lays the foundation for scientific and reflective thinking.

This book aims to: (1) familiarise children with their environment by introducing the variety of birds around them; (2) help build habits of careful observation; (3) stimulate inquiry about the natural world; and (4) develop communication and critical thinking skills. Its use can help children acquire language and mathematical skills by expanding their vocabulary and providing opportunities for classification and measurement.

Project with Observation

Primary science seeks to lead children to explore their environment and describe observations effectively. The birds are described in ways that suggest key features and relationships, thereby stimulating questions. The checklist guides children in making and recording their observations, helping them develop vital information skills. As children learn to observe birds, they are also learning how to learn, and so preparing for lifelong education.

Themes across the Curriculum

Teachers can derive a number of important links to the curriculum. For instance, adaptation to the environment is an important scientific concept, for which birds provide many excellent examples — the relationship between food and habitat, the shape of the bill or type of feet. A basic issue of our time is the relationship between human beings and other living things and the need to conserve the world's resources. Practical ways to apply this principle of environmental education are found in the activities suggested for creating a bird-friendly environment.

AUTHOR

Virginia W Dike is a retired professor of library and information science at the University of Nigeria, specialising in school libraries and children's literature. She helped found the Children's Centre, a model library serving children throughout the Nsukka area: www.childrenscentreunn.org. She grew up watching birds in America and continues to enjoy them in Nigeria. *Birds of Our Land* is her way of sharing this joy with children.

Dedicated to my children –
Ejim, Ije, Nkem, Chinelo, and Chinweze

Revised edition
In memory of my parents,
William B. Weisell and Mary Craig Weisell,
who introduced me to the joys of bird watching

ILLUSTRATOR

Robin Gowen is a contemporary artist living and working in California. She grew up in Nigeria and New Hampshire, and has an intense interest in all elements of the natural world.

For my parents,
Florence and Frederick Gowen,
who gave me my introduction
to Nigeria and its wonders